Daisy Farm Crafts

OUR FAVORITE CROCHET STITCHES

OUR FAVORITE CROCHET STITCHES

By Daisy Farm Crafts

Created by Tiffany Brown and
Hannah Brown McKay

ISBN: 978-0-578-91527-2

INTRODUCTION

Hello! We're Tiffany and Hannah, the mom and daughter behind Daisy Farm Crafts, and this book is a quick reference guide for our favorite crochet stitches!

Since we are often designing baby blankets, we really wanted to create a simple book where we could easily access pictures and instructions of our favorite stitches, and we thought you might enjoy one, too!

We did our best to explain these stitches in a way we hope makes sense, but if you do find yourself needing some more visual help, you can find videos for all the stitches in this book on the Daisy Farm Crafts YouTube Channel.

Feel free to create your own designs with these stitches; they are the ingredients to beautiful crochet and for everyone! Enjoy!

XO, Tiffany and Hannah

SUGARBUSH

CHILL

100% extra fine merino/
mérino extra fine

3.5 oz./100 g

TIPS BEFORE GETTING STARTED

- When counting chains, never count the loop around the hook.

- There are three ways to work into a base chain: the back loop only, the back loop and underneath the back bump, or into the back bump only. It is personal preference as to which way is chosen.

- It's assumed that a stitch is always worked under both little "v's" (into the top of the stitch) unless otherwise stated specifically as back loop only or front loop only.

- Stitch markers are extremely helpful to keeping the sides of the work straight. Place a marker in the first stitch of each row. Upon returning, it will be the last stitch to be worked into. The last stitch worked into becomes the first stitch of the next row.

- Turning chains do not count as a stitch unless noted in the instructions. Usually, turning chains provide height to get up to the next row.

- Find every stitch demonstrated on the Daisy Farm Crafts YouTube Channel Stitches Playlist.

ABBREVIATIONS

(US TERMS)

YO - Yarn Over

CH - Chain

ST - Stitch

SK - Skip

REP - Repeat

SL ST - Slip Stitch

SC - Single Crochet

ESC - Extended Single Crochet

HDC - Half Double Crochet

WHDC - Wide Half Double Crochet

HHDC - Herringbone Half Double Crochet

HBDC - Herringbone Double Crochet

DC - Double Crochet

TC - Treble Crochet

OUR FAVORITE CROCHET STITCHES

BASICS / 10

Single Crochet, Half Double Crochet, Double Crochet, Treble Crochet, Slip Stitch, Half Double Slip Stitch, Herringbone Half Double Crochet, Herringbone Double Crochet (with variations)

COMBOS / 54

Mixed Loop Stitch, Even Mixed Loop Stitch, Griddle Stitch, Crumpled Griddle Stitch, Mesh Stitch, Moss Stitch, Even Moss Stitch, Spider Stitch, Sedge Stitch

CLASSICS / 78

Wattle Stitch, Grit Stitch, Sprig Stitch, Pike Stitch, Modified Daisy Stitch, Linked Stitch, Shell Stitch, Boxed Block Stitch

CLUSTERS & BOBBLES / 96

Wide HDC Cluster, HDC Cluster Across Two Stitches, Berry Stitch, Puff Stitch, Double Crochet Bobble, Crunch Stitch, Double Crochet Post Ribbing

BASICS

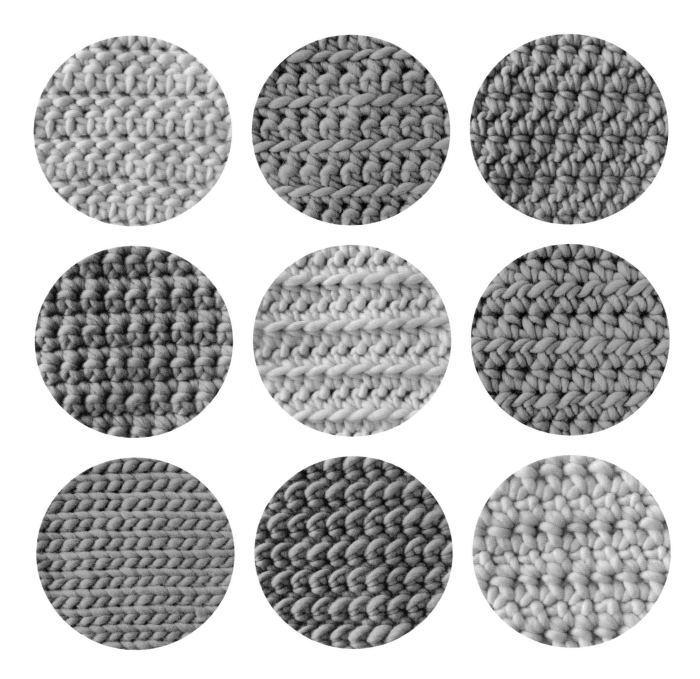

SINGLE CROCHET

Insert your hook, YO and pull up a loop, YO and pull through two loops on hook

---

CHAIN

Any number

ROW 1

Starting in the 2nd chain from the hook, *insert your hook, YO and pull up a loop, YO and pull through two loops on hook. Repeat from * in each chain. CH 1 and turn.

ROW 2

Starting in the 1st stitch, *insert your hook, YO and pull up a loop, YO and pull through two loops on hook. Repeat from * in each stitch to end of row. CH 1 and turn.

REPEAT ROW 2

SINGLE CROCHET (FRONT LOOP)

Insert your hook into front loop, YO and pull up a loop, YO and pull through two loops on hook

---

CHAIN
Any number

ROW 1
Starting in the 2nd chain from the hook, *insert your hook, YO and pull up a loop, YO and pull through two loops on hook. Repeat from * in each chain. CH 1 and turn.

ROW 2
Starting in the 1st stitch, *insert your hook into the front loop, YO and pull up a loop, YO and pull through two loops on hook. Repeat from * in each stitch to end of row. CH 1 and turn.

REPEAT ROW 2

SINGLE CROCHET
(BACK LOOP)

*Insert your hook into back loop, YO and pull up a
loop, YO and pull through two loops on hook*

CHAIN

Any number

ROW 1

Starting in the 2nd chain from the hook, *insert your hook, YO and pull up a loop, YO and pull through two loops on hook. Repeat from * in each chain. CH 1 and turn.

ROW 2

Starting in the 1st stitch, *insert your hook into the back loop, YO and pull up a loop, YO and pull through two loops on hook. Repeat from * in each stitch to end of row. CH 1 and turn.

REPEAT ROW 2

EXTENDED SINGLE CROCHET

*Insert your hook, YO and pull up a loop, YO and pull through one
loop, YO and pull through remaining two loops*

CHAIN

Any number

ROW 1

Starting in the 2nd chain from the hook, *insert your hook, YO and pull up a loop, YO and pull through one loop, YO and pull through remaining two loops. Repeat from * in each chain. CH 1 and turn.

ROW 2

Starting in the 1st stitch, *insert your hook, YO and pull up a loop, YO and pull through one loop, YO and pull through the remaining two loops. Repeat from * in each stitch to end of row. CH 1 and turn.

REPEAT ROW 2

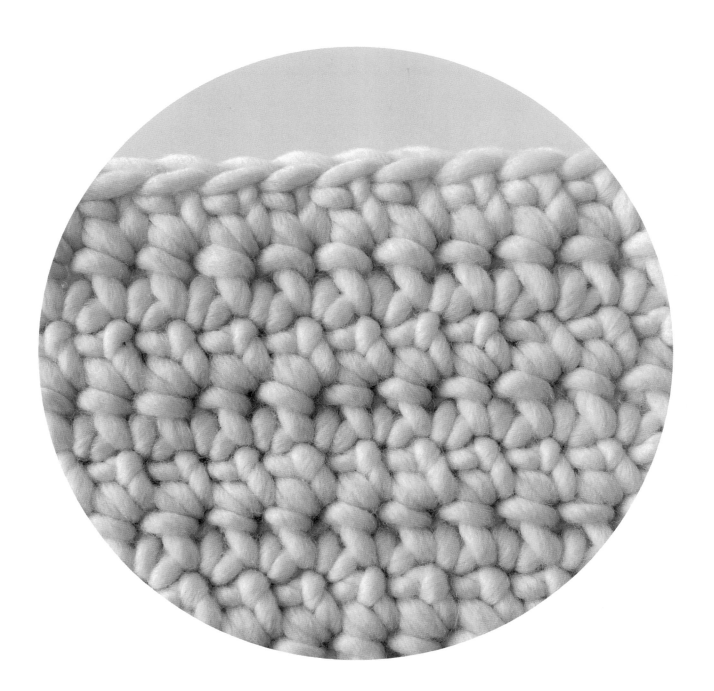

HALF DOUBLE CROCHET

YO, insert your hook, YO and pull up a loop,
YO and pull through all three loops on hook

CHAIN

Any number

ROW 1

Starting in the 3rd chain from the hook, *YO, insert your hook, YO and pull up a loop, YO and pull through all three loops on hook. Repeat from * in each chain. CH 2 and turn.

ROW 2

Starting in the 1st stitch, *YO, insert your hook, YO and pull up a loop, YO and pull through all three loops on hook. Repeat from * in each stitch to end of row. CH 2 and turn.

REPEAT ROW 2

HALF DOUBLE CROCHET (FRONT LOOP)

YO, insert your hook up and under front loop, YO and pull up a loop, YO and pull through all three loops on hook

---

CHAIN
Any number

ROW 1
Starting in the 3rd chain from the hook, *YO, insert your hook, YO and pull up a loop, YO and pull through all three loops on hook. Repeat from * in each chain. CH 2 and turn.

ROW 2
Starting in the 1st stitch, *YO, insert your hook up and under front loop, YO and pull up a loop, YO and pull through all three loops on hook. Repeat from * in each stitch to end of row. CH 2 and turn.

REPEAT ROW 2

HALF DOUBLE CROCHET (BACK LOOP)

YO, insert your hook into back loop, YO and pull up a loop, YO and pull through all three loops on hook

---

CHAIN

Any number

ROW 1

Starting in the 3rd chain from the hook, *YO, insert your hook, YO and pull up a loop, YO and pull through all three loops on hook. Repeat from * in each chain. CH 2 and turn.

ROW 2

Starting in the 1st stitch, *YO, insert your hook into back loop, YO and pull up a loop, YO and pull through all three loops on hook. Repeat from * in each stitch to end of row. CH 2 and turn.

REPEAT ROW 2

HALF DOUBLE CROCHET (FRONT TWO LOOP)

YO, insert your hook up and under front two loops, YO and pull up a loop, YO and pull through all three loops on hook

---

CHAIN

Any number

ROW 1

Starting in the 3rd chain from the hook, *YO, insert your hook, YO and pull up a loop, YO and pull through all three loops on hook. Repeat from * in each chain. CH 2 and turn.

ROW 2

Starting in the 1st stitch, *YO, insert your hook up and under front two loops, YO and pull up a loop, YO and pull through all three loops on hook. Repeat from * in each stitch to end of row. CH 2 and turn.

REPEAT ROW 2

HALF DOUBLE CROCHET (FRONT BOTTOM LOOP)

YO, insert your hook under front bottom loop, YO and pull up a loop, YO and pull through all three loops on hook

---

CHAIN

Any number

ROW 1

Starting in the 3rd chain from the hook, *YO, insert your hook, YO and pull up a loop, YO and pull through all three loops on hook. Repeat from * across the row. CH 2 and turn.

ROW 2

Starting in the 1st stitch, *YO, insert your hook under front bottom loop, YO and pull up a loop, YO and pull through all three loops on hook. Repeat from * to end of row. CH 2 and turn.

REPEAT ROW 2

EXTENDED HALF DOUBLE CROCHET

YO, insert your hook, YO and pull up a loop, YO and pull through one loop, YO and pull through remaining three loops

---

CHAIN

Any number

ROW 1

Starting in the 3rd chain from the hook, *YO, insert your hook, YO and pull up a loop, YO and pull through one loop, YO and pull through remaining three loops. Repeat from * in each chain. CH 2 and turn.

ROW 2

Starting in the 1st stitch, *YO, insert your hook, YO and pull up a loop, YO and pull through one loop, YO and pull through remaining three loops. Repeat from * in each stitch to end of row. CH 2 and turn.

REPEAT ROW 2

WIDE HALF DOUBLE CROCHET

YO, insert your hook in between stitch posts of previous row, YO and pull up a loop, YO and pull through three loops on hook

---

CHAIN

Any number

ROW 1

Starting in the 3rd chain from the hook, *YO, insert your hook, YO and pull up a loop, YO and pull through three loops on hook. Repeat from * in each chain. CH 2 and turn.

ROW 2

Starting in the space between the 1st and 2nd stitch, *YO, insert your hook, YO and pull up a loop, YO and pull through three loops on hook. Repeat from * in each space between stitch posts of previous row, ending with the last stitch between the last HDC post and the turning chain. CH 2 and turn.

REPEAT ROW 2

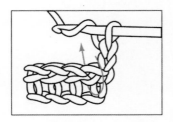

DOUBLE CROCHET

YO, insert your hook, YO and pull up a loop, YO and pull through two loops, YO and pull through remaining two loops

---

CHAIN

Any number

ROW 1

Starting in the 4th chain from the hook, *YO, insert your hook, YO and pull up a loop, YO and pull through two loops, YO and pull through remaining two loops. Repeat from * in each chain. CH 3 and turn. (Turning chain counts as a stitch.)

ROW 2

Starting in the 2nd stitch, *YO, insert your hook, YO and pull up a loop, YO and pull through two loops, YO and pull through remaining two loops. Repeat from * in each stitch to end of row. The last stitch will be worked into the top of the turning chain. CH 3 and turn.

REPEAT ROW 2

DOUBLE CROCHET
(FRONT LOOP)

YO, insert your hook into front loop, YO and pull up a loop, YO and pull through two loops, YO and pull through remaining two loops.

CHAIN
Any number

ROW 1
Starting in the 4th chain from the hook, *YO, insert your hook, YO and pull up a loop, YO and pull through two loops, YO and pull through remaining two loops. Repeat from * in each chain. CH 2 and turn. (Turning chain does not count as a stitch.)

ROW 2
Starting in the 1st stitch, *YO, insert your hook into front loop, YO and pull up a loop, YO and pull through two loops, YO and pull through remaining two loops. Repeat from * in each stitch to end of row. CH 2 and turn.

REPEAT ROW 2

WIDE DOUBLE CROCHET

YO, insert your hook in between stitch posts of previous row, YO and pull up a loop, YO and pull through first two loops on hook, YO and pull through remaining two loops on hook

CHAIN
Any number

ROW 1
Starting in the 3rd chain from the hook, *YO, insert your hook, YO and pull up a loop, YO and pull through first two loops on hook, then YO and pull through remaining two loops on hook. Repeat from * in each chain. CH 2 and turn.

ROW 2
Starting in the space between the 1st and 2nd stitch, *YO, insert your hook, YO and pull up a loop, YO and pull through first two loops on hook, then YO and pull through remaining two loops on hook. Repeat from * in each space between stitch posts of previous row, ending with the last stitch between the last DC post and the turning chain. CH 2 and turn.

REPEAT ROW 2

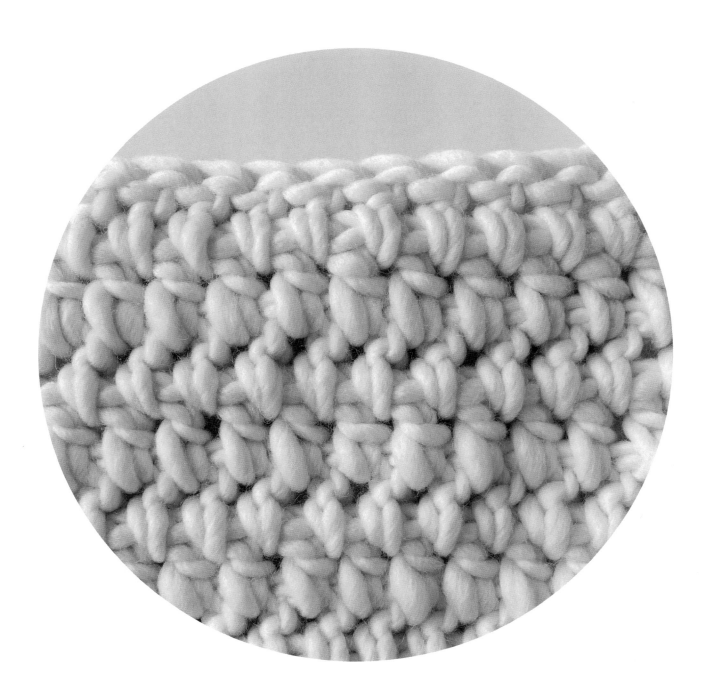

TREBLE CROCHET

YO twice, insert your hook, YO and pull up a loop, YO and pull through two loops, YO and pull through two loops again, YO and pull through remaining two loops

---

CHAIN
Any number

ROW 1
Starting in the 5th chain from the hook, *YO twice, insert hook, YO and pull up a loop, YO and pull through two loops, YO and pull through two loops again, YO and pull through remaining two loops. Repeat from * in each chain. CH 4 and turn. (Turning chain counts as a stitch.)

ROW 2
Starting in the 2nd stitch, *YO twice, insert your hook, YO and pull up a loop, YO and pull through two loops, YO and pull through two loops again, YO and pull through remaining two loops. Repeat from * in each stitch to end of row. The last stitch will be worked into the top of the turning chain. CH 4 and turn.

REPEAT ROW 2

SLIP STITCH
(BACK LOOP)

*Insert your hook into back loop, YO, pull up a
loop and pull directly through loop on hook*

CHAIN
Any number

ROW 1
Starting in the 2nd chain from the hook, *insert your hook, YO, pull up a loop, and pull directly through loop on hook. Repeat from * in each chain. CH 1 and turn.

ROW 2
Starting in the 1st stitch, *insert your hook into back loop only, YO, pull up a loop, and pull directly through loop on hook. Repeat from * in each stitch to end of row. CH 1 and turn.

REPEAT ROW 2

HALF DOUBLE SLIP STITCH

(or Yarn Over Slip Stitch)

*YO, insert your hook, YO, pull up a loop and
pull directly through two loops on hook*

CHAIN

Any number

ROW 1

Starting in the 2nd chain from the hook, *YO, insert your hook, YO, pull up a loop and pull directly through two loops on hook. Repeat from * in each chain. CH 1 and turn.

ROW 2

Starting in the 1st stitch, *YO, insert your hook, YO, pull up a loop and pull directly through two loops on hook. Repeat from * in each stitch to end of row. CH 1 and turn.

REPEAT ROW 2

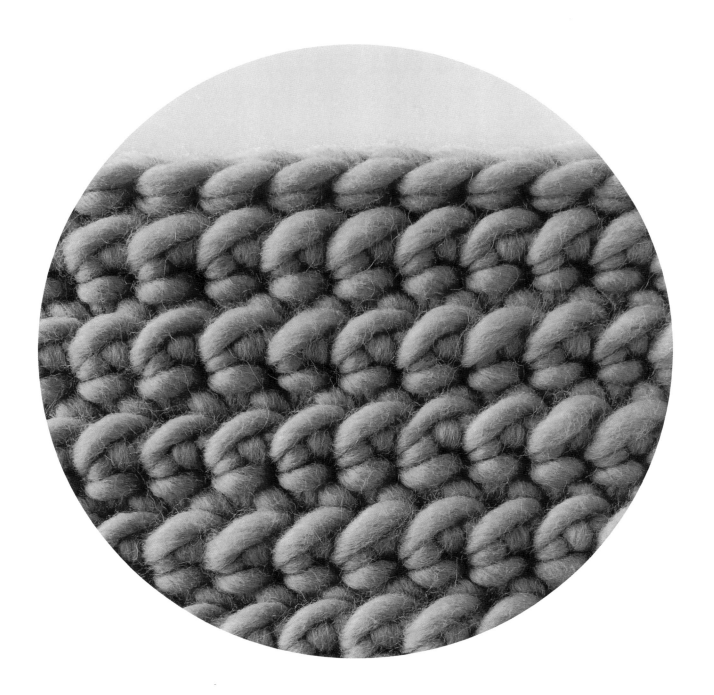

HALF DOUBLE SLIP STITCH (BACK LOOP)

YO, insert your hook into back loop, YO, pull up a loop and pull directly through two loops on hook

---

CHAIN

Any number

ROW 1

Starting in the 2nd chain from the hook, *YO, insert your hook, YO, pull up a loop and pull directly through two loops on hook. Repeat from * in each chain. CH 1 and turn.

ROW 2

Starting in the 1st stitch, *YO, insert hook into back loop, YO, pull up a loop and pull directly through two loops on hook. Repeat from * in each stitch to end of row. CH 1 and turn.

REPEAT ROW 2

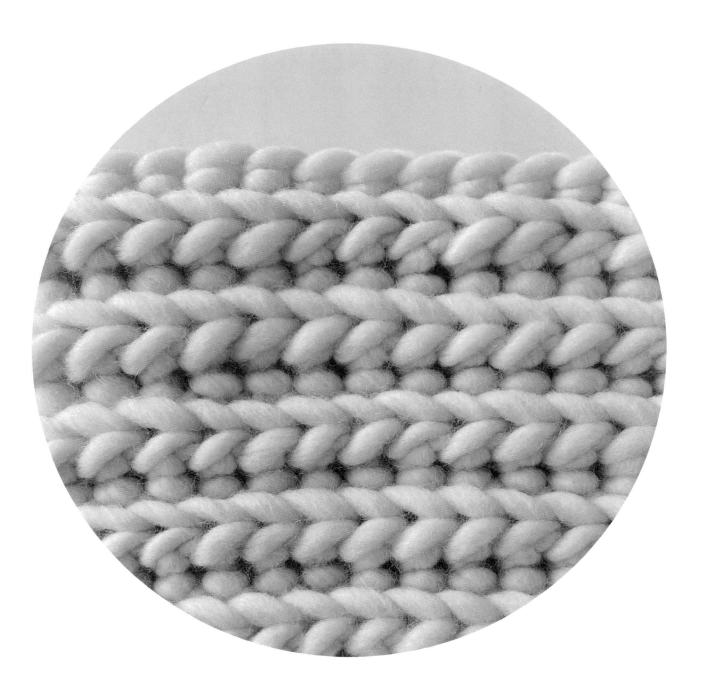

HERRINGBONE HALF DOUBLE CROCHET

YO, insert your hook, YO, pull up a loop and pull directly through first loop on hook, YO and pull through remaining two loops

CHAIN
Any number

ROW 1
Starting in the 3rd chain from the hook, *YO, insert your hook, YO, pull up a loop and pull directly through first loop on hook. YO and pull through remaining two loops. Repeat from * in each chain. CH 2 and turn.

ROW 2
Starting in the 1st stitch, *YO, insert your hook, YO, pull up a loop and pull directly through first loop on hook. YO and pull through the remaining two loops. Repeat from * in each stitch to end of row. CH 2 and turn.

REPEAT ROW 2

HERRINGBONE HALF DOUBLE CROCHET (FRONT LOOP)

YO, insert your hook into front loop, YO, pull up a loop and pull directly through first loop on hook, YO and pull through remaining two loops

---

CHAIN
Any number

ROW 1
Starting in the 3rd chain from the hook, *YO, insert your hook, YO, pull up a loop and pull directly through first loop on hook. YO and pull through remaining two loops. Repeat from * in each chain. CH 2 and turn.

ROW 2
Starting in the 1st stitch, *YO, insert your hook into front loop, YO, pull up a loop and pull directly through first loop on hook. YO and pull through remaining two loops. Repeat from * in each stitch to end of row. CH 2 and turn.

REPEAT ROW 2

HERRINGBONE DOUBLE CROCHET

YO, insert your hook, YO, pull up a loop and pull directly through first loop on hook, YO and pull through one loop, YO and pull through remaining two loops

---

CHAIN
Any number

ROW 1
Starting in the 3rd chain from the hook, *YO, insert your hook, YO, pull up a loop and pull directly through first loop on hook. YO and pull through one loop. YO and pull through remaining two loops. Repeat from * in each chain. CH 2 and turn.

ROW 2
Starting in the 1st stitch, *YO, insert your hook, YO, pull up a loop and pull directly through first loop on hook. YO and pull through one loop. YO and pull through remaining two loops. Repeat from * in each stitch to end of row. CH 2 and turn.

REPEAT ROW 2

COMBOS

MIXED LOOP STITCH

CHAIN
Odd number

ROW 1
Starting in the 3rd chain from the hook, work 1 HDC. 1 HDC in each chain across the row. CH 2 and turn. (Odd number of stitches made.)

ROW 2
Starting in the 1st stitch of the row, *work 1 front bottom loop HDC, then work 1 back loop HDC in the next stitch. Repeat from * to end of row. The last stitch of the row will be a front bottom loop HDC worked into the last stitch. (The turning chain does not count as a stitch.) CH 2 and turn.

REPEAT ROW 2

EVEN MIXED LOOP STITCH

CHAIN
Even number

ROW 1
Starting in the 3rd chain from the hook, work 1 HDC. 1 HDC in each chain across the row. CH 2 and turn. (Even number of stitches made.)

ROW 2
Starting in the 1st stitch of the row, *work 1 front bottom loop HDC, then work 1 back loop HDC in the next stitch. Repeat from * to end of row. The last stitch of the row will be a back loop HDC worked into the last stitch. (The turning chain does not count as a stitch.) CH 2 and turn.

REPEAT ROW 2

HALF DOUBLE CROCHET V-STITCH

CHAIN

Even number

ROW 1

In the 4th chain from hook, work HDC, CH, HDC. *Skip 2 chains, then work HDC, CH, HDC into the next chain. Repeat from * to end of row. Work 1 HDC into the last chain. CH 2 and turn.

ROW 2

In the 1st chain one space of the previous row that is between the HDCs, work HDC, CH 1, HDC. *Skip 2 stitches, then work HDC, CH 1, HDC, into the next chain one space. Repeat from * across the row. End the row with one HDC into the top of the turning chain (or work into space the chain two created if easier). CH 2 and turn.

REPEAT ROW 2

DOUBLE CROCHET V-STITCH

CHAIN
Even number

ROW 1
In the 4th chain from the hook, work 2 DC. Skip the next chain, *2 DC in the next chain space, skip the next chain. Repeat from * across the row until 2 chains left. Skip 1 chain, then 1 DC into the very last chain. CH 3 and turn. (This will count as your first DC.)

ROW 2
Work 2 DC in the space between the second and third DC posts, splitting the pair to form a "V." *Skip 2 stitches, then work 2 DC in between the next pair of DC from previous row. Repeat from * across the row. End row with 1 DC into the top of the turning chain (or work into space the turning chain created if easier). CH 3 and turn.

REPEAT ROW 2

GRIDDLE STITCH

CHAIN

Odd number

ROW 1

Starting in the 2nd chain from hook, *work 1 SC. In the next stitch, work 1 DC. Repeat from * across the row. The last stitch made will be a DC. CH 1 and turn.

ROW 2

Starting in the first stitch, *work 1 SC into the top of the DC of the previous row. 1 DC into the top of the next SC. Repeat from * across the row. The last stitch will be a DC. (Always DC into SC. Always SC into DC.) CH 1 and turn.

REPEAT ROW 2

CRUMPLED GRIDDLE

CHAIN
Even number

ROW 1
Starting in the 2nd chain from hook, *work 1 SC. In the next stitch, work 1 DC. Repeat from * across the row. The last stitch made will be a SC. CH 1 and turn.

ROW 2
Starting in the first stitch, *SC into the top of the SC of the previous row. DC into the next DC. Repeat from * across the row working the final SC into the last SC. (Always DC into DC. Always SC into SC.) CH 1 and turn.

REPEAT ROW 2

MESH STITCH

CHAIN

Even number

ROW 1

Starting in the 2nd chain from the hook, work 1 SC. *CH 1. Skip one chain, SC in next CH, Repeat from * across the row, ending with 1 SC into the last CH. CH 1 and turn.

ROW 2

Starting in the 1st stitch, SC into SC of previous row. *CH 1, skip the chain space, SC into the next SC. Repeat from * across the row, ending with 1 SC into the last SC. CH 1 and turn.

REPEAT ROW 2

MOSS STITCH

CHAIN
Even number

ROW 1
Starting in the 4th chain from hook, work 1 SC. *CH 1. Skip one chain, SC in next chain. Repeat from * across the row, ending with 1 SC into the last CH. CH 2 and turn.

ROW 2
Starting in the first CH 1 space from previous row, work 1 SC. *CH 1, skip 1 SC, SC in next CH 1 space, repeat from * across the row, ending with 1 SC worked into the space between the final SC and turning chain from the previous row. CH 2 and turn.

REPEAT ROW 2

EVEN MOSS STITCH

CHAIN

Even number

ROW 1

Starting in the 2nd chain from hook, *work 1 SL ST (insert your hook, YO, pull up a loop, pull directly through loop on hook). 1 HDC into the next chain. Repeat from * across the row ending with 1 SL ST into the final chain. CH 1 and turn.

ROW 2

Starting in the first stitch, *work 1 SL ST. HDC into the next stitch. Repeat from * across the row, ending with 1 SL ST into the final SL ST. CH 1 and turn. (Always SL ST into a SL ST. Always HDC into a HDC.)

REPEAT ROW 2

SPIDER STITCH

CHAIN

Odd number

ROW 1

In the 3rd chain from the hook, work SC, CH 1, SC. *Skip one chain, then SC, CH 1, SC into the next chain. Repeat from * across the row until 2 chains remain. Skip 1 chain, then end in the final chain with 1 SC. CH 2 and turn.

ROW 2

In the first chain one space of the previous row, work SC, CH 1, SC. *Skip 2 stitches, then work SC, CH 1, SC into the next chain 1 space. Repeat from * across the row ending with 1 SC in the top of the turning chain (or into the space made by the turning chain if that is easier.) CH 2 and turn.

REPEAT ROW 2

SEDGE STITCH

CHAIN
Multiple of 3

ROW 1
In the 2nd chain from the hook, work 1 HDC and 1 DC. *Skip two chains. In the next chain work SC, HDC, DC. Repeat from * across the row until there is one chain left. Work 1 SC into the final chain. CH 1 and turn.

ROW 2
Work 1 HDC and 1 DC into the top of the SC of the previous row. *Skip two stitches, then SC, HDC, DC into the next stitch. Repeat from * across the row ending in the last stitch with 1 SC. CH 1 and turn.

REPEAT ROW 2

CLASSICS

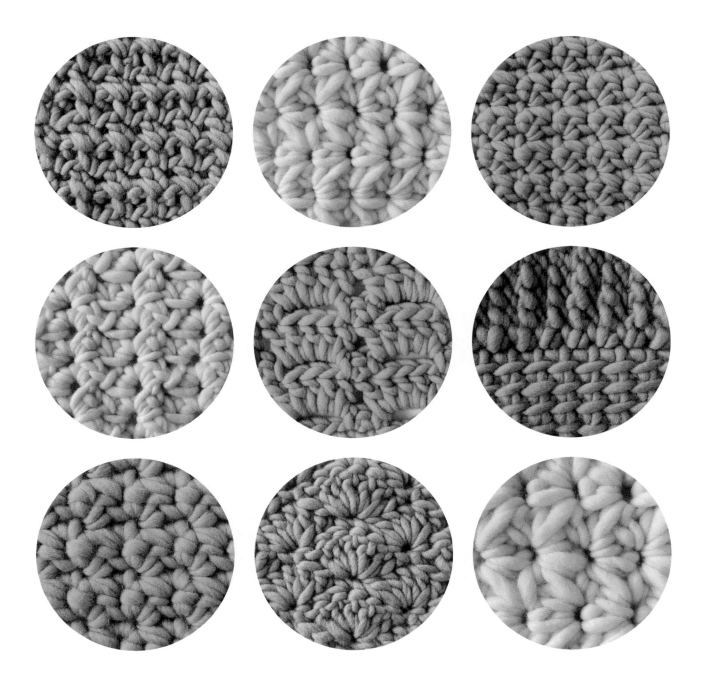

WATTLE STITCH

CHAIN

Multiple of 3

ROW 1

Starting in the 3rd chain from the hook, *work SC, CH 1, DC. Skip two chains. Repeat from * across the row. When 3 chains remain, skip 2 chains and work 1 SC into the last chain. CH 2 and turn.

ROW 2

Skipping the first two stitches, start in the first chain space with *SC, CH 1, DC into the same chain space. Skip two stitches. Repeat from * across the row ending with 1 SC in turning chain. CH 2 and turn.

REPEAT ROW 2

GRIT STITCH

CHAIN

Even number

ROW 1

Starting in the 2nd chain from the hook, work 1 SC. *Skip one chain, work 2 SC into the next chain. Repeat from * across the row ending with 1 SC into the last chain. CH 1 and turn.

ROW 2

Starting in the first stitch, work 1 SC. *Skip 1 SC, work 2 SC into the next stitch. Repeat from * across the row. End with 1 SC into the last SC. CH 1 and turn.

REPEAT ROW 2

SPRIG STITCH

CHAIN
Multiple of 4, plus 3

ROW 1
Starting in the 4th chain from the hook, work 2 SC. CH 2 and in the next chain, work 2 SC. Skip 2 chains, *work 2 SC in the next chain, CH 2, 2 SC in the next chain, skip two chains. Repeat from * until there are 2 chains left. Skip over one and SC into the last chain. CH 3 and turn.

ROW 2
Starting in the first chain 2 space, work 2 SC, 2 CH, 2 SC. *Skip 4 stitches, then work 2 SC, 2 CH, 2 SC into the next chain 2 space. Repeat from * across the row. End with 1 SC in the space formed by the CH 3 turning chain. CH 3 and turn.

REPEAT ROW 2

PIKE STITCH

CHAIN
Odd number

ROW 1
Starting in the 5th chain from the hook, *work 1 extended single crochet (ESC), CH 1, then skip 1 chain. Repeat from * across the row, ending in the last chain with 1 ESC. CH 3 and turn.

ROW 2
Starting in the 2nd stitch, work 1 ESC. *CH 1, skip one, 1 ESC in next stitch. Repeat from * across the row working your last ESC in top of turning chain (or in the space the turning chain made if easier.) CH 3 and turn.

REPEAT ROW 2

MODIFIED DAISY STITCH

CHAIN
Odd number

ROW 1
YO and pull up a loop in the 2nd chain from the hook, YO and pull up a loop in the 3rd chain, YO and skip over the next chain and insert your hook into the next chain and pull up a loop. YO and pull through all 7 loops on your hook. CH 1. *YO and insert your hook into the chain 1 space and pull up a loop, YO and insert your hook into the last chain space you worked into and pull up a loop, YO and skip over the next chain and insert your hook into the next chain and pull up a loop. YO and pull through all 7 loops. CH 1. Repeat from * to the end of the row. CH 3 and turn. (The first chain of the turning chain is the CH 1 that finishes the stitch.)

ROW 2
YO and work into the 2nd chain from the hook and pull up a loop, YO and insert your hook into the next chain and pull up a loop, skip the next stitch, YO and pull up a loop in the next space. YO and pull through all 7 loops. CH 1. *YO and insert your hook into the chain space and pull up a loop, YO and insert your hook into the next space and pull up a loop, skip over one stitch, YO and insert your hook into the next space and pull up a loop. YO and pull through all 7 loops on your hook. Repeat from * to the end of the row, CH 3 and turn.

REPEAT ROW 2

LINKED STITCH

CHAIN

Any number

ROW 1

Starting in the 2nd chain from the hook, insert your hook, yarn over and pull up a loop, *insert your hook into the next chain, yarn over and pull a loop. Repeat from * two more times, (or until desired height of stitch.) Yarn over and pull through two loops 4 times or until you have one loop remaining on the hook.

To begin the next stitch, insert hook under horizontal bar, YO and pull a loop back through. Insert hook under next horizontal bar, YO and pull a loop back through. Continue inserting hook under each horizontal bar in same manner until you reach the chain. Insert hook into next chain, YO and pull a loop back through. Yarn over and pull through 2 loops until one loop remains on hook. CH 4 (or however many you need to match the height on the first row) and turn.

REPEAT ROW 1

SHELL STITCH

CHAIN

Multiple of 6, plus 2

ROW 1

Starting in the 2nd chain from the hook, work 1 SC. *Skip two chains, work 5 DC into the next chain space. Skip two chains, 1 SC into the next chain. Repeat from * across the row ending with 1 SC into the final chain. CH 3 and turn.

ROW 2

Starting in the first stitch, work 2 DC. *Skip 2 stitches, work 1 SC in the next stitch. Skip the next 2 DC, 5 DC in next SC stitch. Repeat from * across the row, ending with 3 DC in the final stitch. CH 1 and turn.

ROW 3

Starting in the first stitch, work 1 SC. *Skip 2 stitches, work 5 DC into the SC, skip 2 stitches, work 1 SC into the next stitch. Repeat from * across ending with 1 SC into the top of the turning chain, CH 3 and turn.

REPEAT ROWS 2 AND 3

BOXED BLOCK STITCH

CHAIN
Multiple of 5, plus 3

ROW 1
Starting in the 2nd chain from the hook, work 1 SC. 1 SC into each CH across the row. CH 1 and turn.

ROW 2
Starting in the 1st stitch, work 1 SC. 1 SC into the next stitch, CH 3. *Skip three stitches, work 1 SC into each of the next two stitches. Repeat from * to the end of the row. CH 3 and turn. (Turning chain counts as a stitch.)

ROW 3
Starting in the space made by the chain 3, work 5 DC. Work 5 DC into each CH 3 space across the row, ending the row with 1 DC into the last SC. CH 1 and turn.

REPEAT ROWS 2 AND 3
Note: The final SC in row 2 will be worked into the top of the turning chain. To finish swatch, work one row of SC.

CLUSTERS
&
BOBBLES

WIDE HALF DOUBLE CROCHET CLUSTER

YO, insert your hook in between stitch posts of previous row, YO and pull up a loop, YO, insert your hook into same space, YO and pull up a loop, YO and pull through all five loops on hook

---

CHAIN
Any number

ROW 1
Starting in the 3rd chain from the hook, *YO, insert your hook, YO and pull up a loop. YO, insert your hook into same space, YO and pull up a loop. YO and pull through all five loops on hook. Repeat from * in each chain to end of row. CH 2 and turn.

ROW 2
Starting in the space between the 1st and 2nd stitch, *YO, insert your hook, YO and pull up a loop. YO, insert your hook into same space, YO and pull up a loop. YO and pull through all five loops on hook. Repeat from * in each space between stitch posts of previous row, ending with the last stitch in between the final stitch post and the turning chain. CH 2 and turn.

REPEAT ROW 2

HALF DOUBLE CROCHET CLUSTER (ACROSS TWO STITCHES)

CHAIN

Any number

ROW 1

Starting in the 3rd chain from the hook, YO and insert your hook, YO and pull up a loop. YO and insert your hook into the next chain, YO and pull up a loop. YO and pull through all five loops on your hook. *YO and insert your hook into the chain space just worked, YO and pull up a loop. YO and insert your hook into the next chain space, YO and pull up a loop. YO and pull through all loops on your hook. Repeat from * to the end of the row. CH 2 and turn.

ROW 2

*YO and insert your hook into the base of the turning chains, (the little hole under the first turning chain) YO and pull up a loop, YO and insert your hook into the next stitch, YO and pull up a loop, YO and pull through all loops on your hook. *YO and insert your hook into the stitch you just worked, YO and pull up a loop, YO and insert your hook into the next stitch, YO and pull up a loop, YO and pull through all loops on your hook. Repeat from * across the row, the last stitch worked into the last stitch of the previous row. (The turning chain does not count as a stitch.) CH 2 and turn.

REPEAT ROW 2

BERRY STITCH

*YO, insert hook, YO and pull up a loop, YO, pull through one loop on hook,
YO, insert hook, YO and pull up a loop, YO, pull through all five loops on hook*

CHAIN
Even number

ROW 1
Starting in the 2nd chain from the hook, work 1 SC. Work 1 SC into each chain across the row. CH 1 and turn.

ROW 2
Starting in the 1st stitch, work 1 SC. In the next stitch, *YO, insert hook, YO and pull up a loop, YO, pull through one loop on hook, YO, insert hook into same stitch, YO and pull up a loop, YO, pull through all five loops on hook. 1 SC into the next stitch. Repeat from * across the row ending with 1 SC into the last stitch. CH 1 and turn.

ROW 3
Starting in the 1st stitch, work 1 SC in each stitch across the row. CH 1 and turn.

REPEAT ROWS 2 AND 3

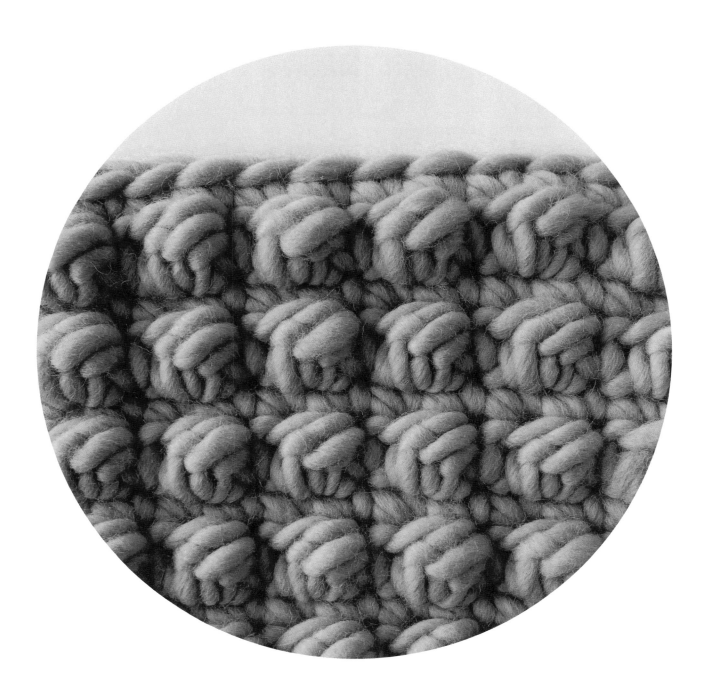

PUFF STITCH

*YO, insert your hook and pull up a loop. Repeat from * 3 more times, inserting your hook into the same space, YO and pull through all loops

---

CHAIN
Even number

ROWS 1 - 3
Starting in the 4th chain from the hook, work 3 rows of Moss Stitch. (see page 70)

ROW 4
Starting in the first chain 1 space, *work 1 puff (*YO, insert your hook and pull up a loop. Repeat from * 3 more times, inserting your hook into the same space, YO and pull through all loops.) CH 1. Repeat from * in each chain 1 space across the row, ending with 1 SC worked in between the last stitch and the turning chain. CH 2 and turn. (In other words, continue working the moss stitch, but substitute each SC for a puff stitch, except on the last stitch of the row.)

ROWS 5 - 7
Work 3 rows of Moss Stitch.

REPEAT ROWS 4 - 7

DOUBLE CROCHET BOBBLE

**YO, insert hook, YO and pull up a loop, YO and pull through 2 loops.
Repeat from * 3 more times, inserting hook into the same space each time.
YO and pull through all loops on hook.*

CHAIN
Multiple of 3, plus 4

ROWS 1 - 3
Starting in the 3rd chain from the hook, work 3 rows of Herringbone Half Double Crochet (HHDC). (See page 48)

ROW 4
Starting in the 1st stitch, work 1 HHDC into each of the first 2 stitches. *1 DC bobble into the next stitch (*YO, insert hook, YO and pull up a loop, YO and pull through 2 loops. Repeat from * 3 more times, inserting hook into the same stitch each time. YO and pull through all loops on hook.) 1 HHDC into each of the next 2 stitches. Repeat from * to the end of the row. CH 2 and turn.

ROWS 5 - 7
Work 3 rows of HHDC.

REPEAT ROWS 4 - 7

CRUNCH STITCH

CHAIN
Even number

ROWS 1 - 3
Starting in the 2nd chain from the hook, work 3 rows of SC.

ROW 4
Starting in the first stitch, *work 1 SC. Work 1 Treble Crochet (TC) into the next stitch (see page 40). Repeat from * across the row ending with 1 SC into the last stitch. CH 1 and turn.

ROWS 5 - 7
Work 3 rows of SC.

REPEAT ROWS 4 - 7

DOUBLE CROCHET POST RIBBING

CHAIN

Even number

ROW 1

Starting in the 4th chain from the hook, work 1 DC. 1 DC into each chain. CH 2 and turn.

ROW 2

Starting with the 2nd post, *work 1 DC around the post by YO and inserting hook from front to back and back to front then complete the DC. (The post pops forward: Front Post DC.) Work 1 DC around next post by YO, inserting hook from back to front and front to back then complete the DC. (Post pops to the back: Back Post DC.) Repeat from * across the row, ending with the last DC worked around the turning chain. CH 2 and turn.

ROW 3

Starting with the 2nd post, *work 1 Front Post DC around the post, then 1 Back Post DC around the next post. Repeat from * to the end of the row, ending with the last DC worked under the turning chain. CH 2 and turn.

REPEAT ROW 3

Thank you for being our crochet friends!
xo, Tiffany and Hannah

Find all of our free crochet patterns on
daisyfarmcrafts.com

Follow us on Instagram, Facebook and Pinterest
@daisyfarmcrafts

Find all of our free video tutorials on the
Daisy Farm Crafts YouTube Channel

Printed in Great Britain
by Amazon

44680689R00066